"Our lives are the rising and falling of a passing wave on the eternal ocean which, in truth we are."
—Issa Das

A NOTE FROM DEMI

For background material on Christopher Columbus, I read hundreds of books, including *Columbus: For Gold, God, and Glory* by John Dyson, Simon & Schuster, New York, 1991; *Columbus and the Age of Discovery* by Zvi Dor-Ner, William Morrow and Co., New York, 1991; Admiral of the Ocean Sea: A Life of Christopher Columbus by Samuel Eliot Morison, Little Brown and Co., Boston, 1942; and *The Diario of Christopher Columbus's First Voyage to America, 1492–1493*, translated by Oliver Dunn and James E. Kelley, Jr., University of Oklahoma Press, 1989. I also read books on tying knots, sailing, and fifteenth-century navigation and watched various films, such as *The Magnificent Voyage of Christopher Columbus*, directed by Zvi Dor-Ner, PBS, 2007. I prepared the artwork with Chinese paintbrushes and inks, gold overlays, and Italian marbled paper from Florence, Italy. There were many diverse and fascinating aspects to Columbus's life, and I loved researching and painting every inch!

I would like to acknowledge the following sources for quotes in the text:
"God granted me the gift of knowledge," on the copyright page and "gods who had been carried ashore," on page 31, *The Log of Christopher Columbus*, translated by Robert H. Fuson, Camden, Maine, International Marine Publishing, October 1987; "No one knows what is in that sea" on page 28, Muhammad al-Idrisi, *The Book of Pleasant Journeys into Faraway Lands (Tabula Rogeriana)*, Rome, 1592; "Columbus had said" on page 58 from the film *The Magnificent Voyage of Christopher Columbus*, directed by Zvi Dor-Ner, PBS, 2007; Christopher Columbus's signature on page 58 from *Columbus: For Gold, God, and Glory* by John Dyson, Simon & Schuster, New York, 1991.

Thanks to Dr. Thomas C. Tirado, Professor Emiritus, History Department, Millersville University of Pennsylvania, for evaluating the text and artwork.

LIBRARY OF CONGRESS CATALOGING-IN-PUBLICATION DATA
Demi. Christopher Columbus / by Demi.
p. cm. ISBN 978-0-7614-6167-8 (hardcover) – ISBN 978-0-7614-6168-5 (ebook)
1. Columbus, Christopher–Juvenile literature. 2. Explorers–America–Biography–
Juvenile literature. 3. Explorers–Spain–Biography–Juvenile literature.
4. America–Discovery and exploration–Spanish–Juvenile literature.
I. Title. E111.D44 2012 970.01'5092--dc23 [B] 2011036019

The illustrations are rendered in mixed media.
Book design by Michael Nelson   Editor: Margery Cuyler
Printed in China (W)   First edition
1 3 5 6 4 2

COLUMBUS

"God granted me the gift of knowledge . . .
and revealed to me that it was feasible
to sail . . . to the Indies, and placed in me
a burning desire to carry out this plan."

—*Christopher Columbus*

WRITTEN AND ILLUSTRATED BY
DEMI

AMAZON
CHILDREN'S
PUBLISHING

N 1451 Christopher Columbus was born to Susanna and Domenico Columbus in Genoa, Italy. His father was a weaver, and young Christopher helped comb the sheep's wool before his father spun it into cloth. Christopher had three younger brothers, Bartolomeo, Giovanni, and Giacomo, and a sister named Bianchinetta.

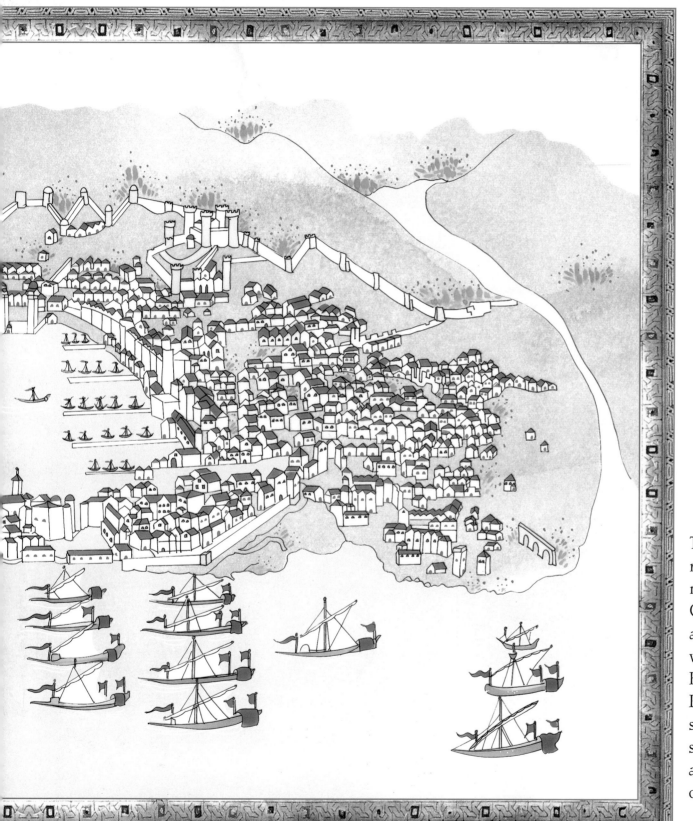

They all learned to weave, read, write, and do simple mathematics. But often Christopher skipped school and ran to the docks to watch the ships arrive from Egypt, Spain, England, and Belgium. Christopher was so fascinated by the sailors' stories of adventure, treasure, and pirates that he dreamed of going to sea.

So strong was the call of the sea that at the age of fourteen, Christopher left home and became a sailor. Quickly he learned about vessels and riggings, wind and stars, currents and tides, maps and sea charts, and he even made maps himself!

He became an expert in the art and practice of navigation, and he sailed all around the Mediterranean along the western coast of Africa.

Columbus developed a profound understanding of weather and prevailing winds, of islands and shorelines, and of the ocean itself. He correctly predicted storms and used the sounding line and the mariner's compass. He read charts and calculated the time-speed distance that is basic knowledge for all sailors.

He sharpened his natural powers of observation, studying the stars and the passage of the sun through the twelve hours of the zodiac. He traced meteors and planets and said, "Navigation is an art which inclines him who follows it to wish to know the secrets of the world."

In August 1476, Columbus was shipwrecked off the coast of Portugal. He struggled ashore and lived among sailors and explorers. Columbus learned to speak Portuguese and Spanish, and he read *The Travels of Marco Polo*. He agreed with Polo that it was possible to reach Asia and the East by sailing west around the Earth.

He imagined the great riches of gold, silk, and ivory that could be gained in trade with Asia. He believed in the great palaces of Kublai Khan. In 1477 Columbus sailed for Southampton, England. From the English port of Bristol, he sailed to Iceland and as far north as Jan Mayen Island, above the Arctic Circle.

Columbus returned to Lisbon, Portugal, to help his brother Bartolomeo make marine charts. There were people who thought the world was flat and that you sailed right off the edge into a dark abyss. They called the Atlantic Ocean "The Sea of Darkness."

"No one knows what is in that sea, because of many obstacles to navigation—profound darkness, high waves, frequent storms, innumerable monsters . . . and violent winds. No sailor dares to penetrate it; they limit themselves to sailing along the coasts without losing sight of land."

—TWELFTH CENTURY
ARAB GEOGRAPHER AL-IDRISI

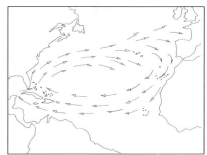

But after so much extensive sailing, Columbus had developed his own secret plan: He would discover the route to the East by sea, and he would travel east by sailing west from Europe, since he had discovered the great oceanic wind system: the northeasterly winds would carry him out, and the westerly winds would carry him home.

In 1479 Columbus fell in love and married the noble woman Felipa Perestrello Moniz, who had access to the Portuguese Court. In 1480 their son, Diego, was born.

They first lived on the island of Madeira, where Columbus became wealthy by trading gold as he sailed up and down the North African coast.

Although busy as a trader, Columbus had not forgotten his plan to sail west to Asia. In 1481 he asked King John II of Portugal to provide him with ships and men to cross the Atlantic Ocean in search of Cipangu (Japan) and India, to bring Christianity to the people, to bring great wealth and power to Portugal, and to make her ruler of all the seas.

The king consulted with his astronomers and mathematicians, who advised against the expedition. They told the king correctly that the Atlantic Ocean was far greater than Columbus had described.

Determined to find another sponsor, Columbus sailed for Spain in 1485. Once there, he was hopeful that King Ferdinand and Queen Isabella would support his plan. He traveled to the monastery at La Rabida, where he met the great astronomer-priest Fray Antonio de Marchena, who shared his scientific discoveries with him.

Columbus's son, Diego, accompanied him, as his mother had died prior to their move, and Columbus thought his sister, who lived in Spain, could help raise the child. While in Spain, Columbus met a peasant and orphan named Beatriz Enríquez de Arana, and together they had a son named Ferdinand. They never married, however, as it was unsuitable for Columbus, an admiral, to marry a commoner.

During this time, King Ferdinand and Queen Isabella were crusading against Islam, determined to drive all Muslims out of Spain so that it would become a totally Christian nation. They also needed to raise money, since Muslims had blocked the land trade routes to the East and its lucrative spice trade. The queen listened to Columbus's plan and asked him to present it to the Royal Committee.

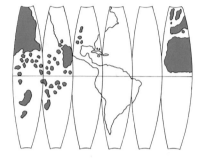

The Committee, however, rejected Columbus's ideas. How could Columbus's statements be true? No one had actually proved the world was round, and such ideas were against the teachings in the Bible. And, like the Portuguese, the Committee was sure the great Atlantic Ocean was much wider than Columbus had described. Again and again Columbus appeared before the Committee, but again and again he was met with skepticism and ridicule, and finally he was dismissed.

Eventually, however, Columbus's luck changed. A monk named Fray Juan Perez intervened on his behalf. Close to the queen, Brother Perez persuaded Isabella to meet with Columbus after the Muslims were driven from Spain. On January 6, 1492, King Ferdinand and Queen Isabella took possession of the city of Granada and won their crusade against the Muslims.

In a grand triumphal procession, Columbus entered the city beside the monarchs. Shortly after, on April 17, 1492, King Ferdinand and Queen Isabella announced Columbus was to have three ships equipped for his expedition so "that he might go and make discoveries and prove true the words he had spoken!"

Martin Alonso Pinzon

On August 3, 1492,
Columbus and his three
ships, the Niña, the Pinta, and
the Santa Maria, left Spain for
the vast unknown. The ship's
crew numbered about ninety
men, including one doctor,
a silversmith, an Arabic
interpreter, carpenters, monks,
envoys of the Spanish Court,
and many volunteer sailors.

Vincent Yañez Pinzon

Two wealthy merchant brothers from Palos, Spain, were appointed captains of two of the ships. Martin Alonso Pinzon took charge of the Pinta, Vincent Yañez Pinzon of the Niña, and Columbus became captain of the third and largest ship, the Santa Maria.

Columbus began his voyage, swinging south toward the Canary Islands, and then headed directly west on the nineteenth or twentieth parallel. Columbus said, "We do not know for certain that anyone has passed this course until the present time!"

The three small ships sailed on and on and seemed all alone on a great forbidding ocean. The sailors grew restless and panicked when they came to the green Sargasso Sea choked with seaweed. They thought they would never see land again. Columbus assured them they would, and that in the end they would gain honor and glory for partaking in the marvelous discovery of a sea route to Asia. Still, the sailors were terrified of the great expanse of the sea. They were also terrified that their food would run out and they would all starve to death. Columbus tried to inspire them with visions of the riches and gold that lay ahead, and he invoked the mercy of God.

Weeks passed. A little crayfish was found in some weeds—a sure sign of land! Then a tunny fish, a ringtail bird, two pelicans, and a jay were spotted. A whale swam by, and little birds and sandpipers began to settle and sing on the riggings. A piece of sugarcane and a branch with roseberries were sighted.

On October 11, 1492, at 10 p.m., Columbus thought he saw a light, and a sailor cried out, "Light! LAND!", but a mist settled on the water, and it was too dark to see anything clearly. However, at dawn on October 12, 1492, after two months at sea over a distance of 2,121 miles, the mist suddenly lifted, and there before everyone's eyes was LAND! The men saw an island with green grass, rocks, trees, and a great blue lake! They all rejoiced and thanked God.

A boat was quickly lowered from the Santa Maria, and Columbus was rowed ashore. Great numbers of native Indians rushed to greet him, amazed by the "gods who had been carried ashore by strange white birds."

Thinking he had reached Eastern Asia, Columbus called the natives "Indios." In fact, they were Tainos, members of the Arawak tribes that lived in Central America. Columbus wore a bright scarlet coat over his shining steel armor, and he towered above everyone. The two Pinzon brothers carried the banners of King Ferdinand and Queen Isabella. All the men fell to their knees and kissed the ground for joy, thanking God for his great mercy. They sang, "Gloria in excelsis Deo! Glory to God in the highest!"

Columbus drew his sword and took possession of the land, calling it San Salvador, "Holy Savior," in honor of Jesus Christ.

Still intent on finding Japan (Cipangu), Columbus and his crew sailed south in November 1492, exploring the Caribbean and claiming many islands for Isabella and Ferdinand, including the Bahamas, Hispaniola, Jamaica, and Cuba. Cuba was so big that Columbus thought he had landed in China. Everywhere he went, the natives were friendly and they all spoke the same language. But there was not much gold, few pearls, no ivory or any silks, and certainly not the great palaces of the Great Khan. There were dyes, spices, tobacco, and medicines. Exotic animals and birds like lizards and parrots were everywhere. And the sailors enjoyed the native habit of sleeping in a swinging bed or hammock.

On November 21, 1492,
Martin Alonso Pinzon,
captain of the Pinta,
mutinied. He sailed north in
search of gold and glory for
himself. Columbus, on the
Santa Maria, and Vincent
Yañez Pinzon on the
Niña continued exploring
Hispaniola, sailing close to
the coastline and hoping
to discover more riches.

Then on Christmas Eve, December 24, 1492, disaster struck. It was late at night and all the sailors were tired. Columbus had gone to sleep, when suddenly the ship's boy screamed.

The Santa Maria had struck
a coral reef! Holes had torn
the ship's hull, water was
pouring in, and the Santa
Maria was sinking!

Nothing could be done,
as the waves drove the
crippled vessel further onto
the rocks. Columbus barely
had time to escape to shore
with his men.

With wood that he salvaged from the Santa Maria, Columbus and his men built a fort called La Navidad. Then, leaving thirty-nine volunteers at the fort with a years' supply of wine, grain, and bread, Columbus made plans to return to Spain with the rest of his men on the Pinta, which by now had returned with little gold. Seven Tainos would also go on the voyage, as Columbus believed that their gentle ways would make it easy to convert them to Christianity. In fact, he had disrespected their culture and treated them as no more than slaves.

On January 16, 1493, the
Niña and the Pinta sailed
for home. As the expedition
departed, a tribe of local
Indians, the Ciguayos,
attacked the ships with
bows and arrows. Their
faces were blackened with
charcoal and their hair was
decorated with parrot
feathers. The Spaniards fired
back with guns, hitting two
Indians, and causing the rest
to flee in disarray.

Catching the prevailing eastward winds, the ships headed home. On February 13, 1493, Columbus "experienced great difficulty with the wind, high waves and a stormy sea." Lightning flashed across the skies, and a dark and violent hurricane pounded the two little ships. Certain that his ships would sink, Columbus wrote a secret note of his discoveries to King Ferdinand and Queen Isabella, which he sealed in waxed cloth inside a barrel and threw overboard. When the storm broke, Columbus sailed straight to the Portuguese Azores. The Portuguese governor, ignorant of Columbus's mission, arrested many of the men. Only after Columbus showed his official papers from the Spanish Crown and threatened to "shoot up the town" did the government release the prisoners.

With fresh provisions, Columbus set off on the last leg of his journey home. But violent storms struck again, and once more Columbus had to find shelter in Portuguese territory. He sailed up the River Tagus to Lisbon and could have been arrested, but instead, the Portuguese king, John II, listened to Columbus's story and only regretted he had not sponsored Columbus in the first place. "Why did I let slip such a wonderful chance?" he said.

On March 15, 1493, Columbus reached the Spanish port of Palos, where King Ferdinand and Queen Isabella gave him a splendid hero's welcome.

This was the greatest moment of his life:

He had accomplished a great feat of seamanship.

He had reached distant lands, and he had claimed them for Isabella and Ferdinand. He "said" he had reached the Indies, and he greatly exaggerated the riches of the land. He was honored with a coat of arms and appointed Admiral of the Ocean Sea and Governor of the lands he had explored.

All the men who had sailed with him joined in the triumphal procession. Indians in plumed headdresses with fishbone and gold ornaments marched along, as did natives carrying parrots and pelicans on streaming banners, while bands of boys played trumpets and drums.

A second and greater voyage was quickly planned. On September 25, 1493, Columbus departed from Cadiz for the New World. This time, his expedition was made up of 17 ships and 1,200 men. Besides sailors, there were cavalry troops, farmers, Spanish aristocrats, a physician, and six priests. Columbus sailed further south on a new ship, also named the Santa Maria, in hopes of reaching the Asian mainland.

On November 27, 1493, Columbus landed on an island that he named Dominica ("Lord God"). He then explored what are now called the Virgin Islands and Puerto Rico. When the Carib Indians attacked and killed one of his men on Saint Croix, Columbus decided to head north to the fort at La Navidad. Upon landing, he was shocked to discover that the colony no longer existed and that all the men were dead. The Indians, angered by the way the Spanish mistreated them, had razed La Navidad and murdered all thirty-nine Spaniards.

Columbus did not mourn for long. He founded a second colony and named it La Isabella after the queen. Next he explored the coast of Cuba and the island of Jamaica, all the time searching for gold. By now his men had grown weary. They questioned his leadership; Columbus had said the Indians were friendly, yet they had slaughtered the men at La Navidad; the colony was to be Spanish, but Columbus was Italian; Columbus said they would find gold, but there was little, and no other riches. However, there were mosquitoes, yellow fever, and malaria. Jungle dampness rotted their food, and no fields were being planted, since everyone was searching for gold. Supplies were dwindling and the men were threatened with starvation. Queen Isabella and King Ferdinand, alarmed by the reports they were hearing, sent several relief ships to the Indies.

One of the captains was Christopher Columbus's brother Bartolomeo. Upon arrival, he discovered that the Spaniards were exploiting the Indians. They were stealing from them, had cut off the ears of one man, and had put the Indian chief in chains. Violence spread and Columbus could not stop it. Columbus sent back four ships to Spain with five hundred Taino Indians who were sold as slaves on the European market. And he continued to practice slavery in the Indies.

Every male over the age of fourteen had to pay gold every three months to the shaky government Columbus had set up. The males were forced to work for the Spaniards after giving up their land and belongings. Many began to die of exhaustion and European diseases, including smallpox, measles, and syphilis. Soon hundreds of thousands of Caribbean Indians died, and eventually only a handful survived.

Upon hearing of these disasters, in 1495 King Ferdinand and Queen Isabella summoned Columbus back to Spain. Before he returned, the monarchs wanted him to convert the native Tainos to Christianity and not keep them as slaves. The King and Queen ordered Columbus to free the slaves and asked him to explain why he had made them slaves in the first place. Columbus wrote back, assuring them of future successes. He had explored seven hundred islands, he claimed.

"But where was the gold, the spices, and the great wealth you promised?" asked the monarchs.

"They will come! I promise!" assured Columbus.

Columbus did not set sail for Spain until March 1496. Leaving his brother Bartolomeo in charge of the colony, he took two hundred Indians with him on the Niña. It was a miserable, overcrowded voyage. Food ran out and some of the men even suggested eating the Indians. When the boat finally landed, people on shore were stunned to see half-starved Spaniards looking like skeletons. Wearing the robes of a Franciscan friar, Columbus stepped down from the ship, pleading poverty and displaying his Christian faith for all to see. The Royal Court mocked and humiliated Columbus, calling him "The Admiral of Mosquitoes." The king and queen were critical and offered to pay him an annual salary if he would retire and not return to his colony. Columbus refused, believing the land he had discovered was his. He wanted to return to the Indies to finish his explorations.

On May 30, 1498, Columbus left the Spanish port of Lucar on his third expedition. He arrived in Trinidad two months later and explored the coast of South America. Landing on Venezuela's Paria Penninsula, he became the first European explorer to set foot on the American mainland since the Vikings five centuries earlier. The land was so beautiful, Columbus was sure he had reached The Garden of Eden.

Columbus was also convinced that the Court of Kublai Khan was just around the corner, and now scientists, explorers, and church officials were beginning to believe that Columbus had found more than he had even dreamed of, the vast lands of what are now North, Central, and South America.

Events, however, were beginning to spiral out of control for Christopher Columbus. The new colony in Santo Domingo, Hispaniola, was governed by his brother Bartolomeo, who had abandoned Española in Christopher's absence. The colonists were about to rebel because of total mismanagement. Columbus could rule the sea, but not the land. In the summer of 1500, King Ferdinand and Queen Isabella sent Judge Francisco de Bobadilla to assess the situation. The judge was shocked to find Christopher and Bartolomeo absent, exploring for gold, and seven colonists hanging for their crimes and five more awaiting execution.

As soon as the Columbus brothers returned, Judge Bobadilla placed them in chains, declared them guilty of mismanagement, and ordered them to stand trial in Spain.

At his trial in Spain, Columbus looked like an old man. His hair was white, his eyes were inflamed, and he suffered from temporary blindness. He walked with difficulty due to extensive rheumatism. He had to wait nine months before his case was decided: Columbus could keep his titles, but he could never return to Hispaniola. A new governor was chosen in his place. The monarchs offered Columbus money on which to retire, a castle, and provisions for the rest of his life.

But Columbus would not retire. He begged the monarchs for more ships so he could continue to search for the riches of the Orient. He knew they were there! Wearily, King Ferdinand and Queen Isabella granted him four small and rickety ships.

In the spring, on May 11, 1502, Columbus set sail with a crew of 140, many only boys, and his twelve-year-old son Ferdinand. In only three weeks, he reached the island of Martinique, then headed straight for Hispaniola, even though he had been forbidden to do so. A hurricane was brewing and he asked the governor to shelter his ships, but the governor laughed in his face. The governor had already organized a naval expedition of his own—twenty-six ships that were ready to sail for Spain. That night twenty-five of his ships sank in the storm, and only one reached Spain—the one carrying gold!

For more than a year, Columbus explored the rivers and inlets of the Caribbean, Panama, and Central America. He continued to search for a sea passage to the West and the riches of the East, but he found only bits of gold, lots of trouble, and many disappointments.

By June 1503 Columbus was forced to beach his worm-eaten ships on the coast of Jamaica, where he and his crew remained stranded for more than a year. Two men were selected to try to reach Hispaniola in two canoes lashed together with a sail. On shore, Columbus had to deal with mutiny, chaos, and starvation.

To demonstrate his great powers to the Indians so they would supply his men with food, Columbus correctly predicted an eclipse of the moon, which he knew would happen because of what was predicted in his almanac. When the eclipse occurred and the moon got darker and darker, the natives panicked and promised Columbus all the food he needed if he would stop the moon from disappearing. Finally, in June 1504, a rescue ship arrived to take Columbus and his men back to Spain.

Columbus returned home on November 7, 1504, after crossing the Atlantic Ocean for the eighth time. Before the end of the year, Queen Isabella died and King Ferdinand refused to see Columbus. He was tired of Columbus's urgent demands for rights and privileges for himself and his sons.

In his old age Columbus became increasingly devout, claiming to hear divine voices and preaching that the end of the world was near.

Columbus, crippled by arthritis, died in Valladolid, Spain, at the age of fifty-four, on May 20, 1506. Later, he was re-buried at the monastery of La Cartuja in Seville, but no one from the Spanish court attended. However, Columbus's travels were not over. In 1542 he was taken by ship across the Atlantic to Hispaniola and buried in the new church, the Cathedral of Santo Domingo.

Then, in 1795, he was re-buried in Havana, Cuba. In 1895, he crossed the Atlantic once more to Spain and was interred in the Cathedral of Seville. To this day, scholars continue to dispute where Columbus really lies.

Columbus had said, "Life has more imagination than we carry in our dreams!"

Columbus imagined sailing west to reach the East; he imagined reaching China and all the riches of Kublai Khan; he imagined all the possibilities that lay over the horizon.

He died a magnificent failure. Columbus, the tyrant, had destroyed the Taino culture and enslaved the islanders. Yet he was one of the greatest navigators who ever lived. He had not reached the Orient, yet he had established a firm foothold on the continent of America, and his voyages had changed the face of the world forever!

.S.
.S. A .S.
X M Y
—
X͡ρο FERENS

"I AM THE SERVANT OF
THE MOST HIGH SAVIOR"
"CHRIST, MARY AND JESUS"
"EXCELLENT,
MAGNIFICENT,
ILLUSTRIOUS."

NORTH ATLANTIC OCEAN

GULF
OF
MEXICO

FLORIDA

CUBA

SARGASSO SEA

LA NAVIDAD
LA ISABELA

JAMAICA

ESPANOLA

SAN JUAN

SANTO DOMINGO

CARIBBEAN
SEA

DOMINICA

HONDURAS

NICARAGUA

TRINIDAD

PANAMA

COLUMBIA

VENEZUELA

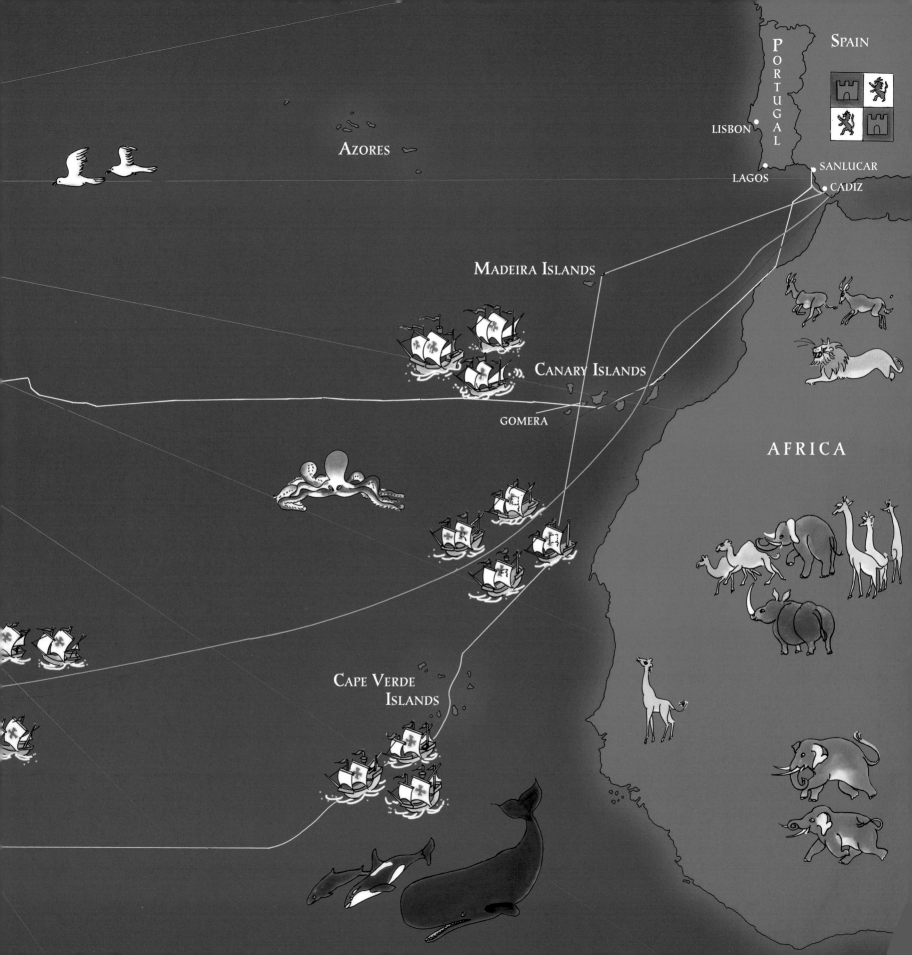